TIGHT LINES
&
GOOD SELLING

Business Growth Lessons Learned at the Point of a Hook

Jon Wright

Published by
Innovo Publishing, LLC
www.innovopublishing.com
1-888-546-2111

Providing Full-Service Publishing Services for
Christian Authors, Artists & Organizations: Hardbacks, Paperbacks,
eBooks, Audiobooks, Music & Film

**TIGHT LINES AND GOOD SELLING:
BUSINESS GROWTH LESSONS LEARNED AT THE POINT OF A HOOK**

Copyright © 2016 Jon Wright
All rights reserved.

No part of this publication may be reproduced, stored in a retrieval system, or transmitted in any form or by any means electronic, mechanical, photocopying, recording, or otherwise, without the prior written permission of the author.

Library of Congress Control Number: 2016941410
ISBN: 978-1-61314-332-2

Cover Design & Interior Layout: Innovo Publishing, LLC

Printed in the United States of America
U.S. Printing History
First Edition: June 2016

TABLE OF CONTENTS

1. Flashback 5
2. Check Your Fly 25
3. Thumpin' the Lid 39
4. Eliminate the Dead Water 49
5. Match the Hatch 59
6. Time and Tide Wait for No Man 65
7. The Men of 1000 Casts 73
8. Don't Be a Poser 81
9. The Big Catch 89
10. A Final Cast from the Author 93

About the Author 97

CHAPTER 1
FLASHBACK

Taylor worked hard in college, and she had fun. She managed to graduate with a high GPA and earn her undergraduate degree in communications in four years at a major university. She also earned "cum laude" honors in sorority life, never missing an opportunity to mix, mingle, and laugh her way through any social activity that was available on or near campus.

After graduation, her goal was to use her interpersonal skills and competitive nature to land a job in sales. She sent out countless copies of her resume, contacted anyone and everyone that could help her gain an interview, and had more "let's get together for coffee or lunch" meetings than she could count. As a result of her faith, persistence, and relentless drive to reach a personal goal, she was eventually hired by a pharmaceutical manufacturer and would relocate to a midsized city that she had never visited or even thought about.

Her new employer provided tremendous resources in terms of product knowledge, sales literature, and expectations. But they offered little when it came to the actual planning and strategy. After three weeks of in-house training, she had a strong knowledge of her product line, her competition, and what was expected of her concerning her bottom-line sales results. She was pumped and ready to rip. Now it was time to sell.

On the Sunday evening before the first day of being "unleashed" in her new territory, a wave of terror hit Taylor right between the ears. She began to panic. Her pores opened up and sweat started to glisten.

What am I doing? she thought. *I don't know how to do this or where to begin.*

She possessed a ton of account notes and spreadsheets that her manager had provided but had no clue of what to do with them.

Where am I actually going to go, who am I going to see, and what am I going to say? On top of that, how in the world am I going to produce enough results to earn a bonus?

Her brain was racing and her thoughts about tomorrow were crashing together. It was ridiculously bad. Then, for some reason, she thought about the fishing trips with her dad.

♪♪♪

When Taylor was a little girl—before smartphones, the freedom provided by her driver's license, and discovering boys (and boys discovering her)—she would often go fishing with her dad. Those two went on many types of trips, from fishing for bream with crickets and worms on a small farm pond, casting for rainbow trout in cool mountain streams, to cruising the inshore and nearshore depths of the ocean hoping to catch anything and everything that might bite. They both loved it. She had fun messing around with the bait, spotting the different types of wildlife, and feeling the pull of a fish on the end of her line. Her father enjoyed those things too, but he also got a huge kick out of making memories and spending time with his little girl.

The time leading up to a "serious" fishing trip was almost ritualistic for her dad. It was all about the preparation. Days, sometimes weeks, before every fishing trip, her dad would always put a game plan together. He would check and recheck all of the tackle to make sure that everything worked smoothly, spool the reels with new line, and gather and pack ever type of lure, hook, and weight needed to seduce the fish that they were planning to catch. Everything—rods, reels, lures/bait, sunscreen, insect repellant, food and drink—was ready to go the night before the trip.

"Better to have and not need than need and not have," he would say.

Taylor's dad, who she playfully called "Pops," had a knack for packing just the right amount—not too much so that things would get in the way, but not too little so that it would affect the trip if they didn't have anything.

"Come here, kiddo. Let me show you something," he would say. He would point at different places on the maps and aerial photos of the area that they were going to fish. (This was before computer-displayed maps and GPS coordinates were as available and easy to use as they are now.)

"See how light most of the water looks except in these four places? That means that these dark places are either deeper than the rest of the area or that some type of grass or structure is underneath that water. Find the changes in depth and the structure and you'll find the baitfish. Find the baitfish, and you'll find the big fish. I bet we catch something there," he'd say with a grin. "We're going to start in this area and then move to the different spots that I've highlighted later on in the day as the conditions change. You'll use the rod and reel that you usually use, and I've tied on a magic lure that will be i-r-r-e-s-t-i-b-l-e to the fish!"

It could be argued that her dad got as much enjoyment out of preparing to fish as actually going fishing.

Early in the morning on the day of the trip, Taylor's father would wake her up, give her a Pop-Tart, and guide her groggy steps into the family SUV and head to the water.

It didn't matter what type of fishing they were doing or what type of fish they were trying to catch; they usually met their goal of catching something, and they always had a great time trying.

༄༄༄

The flashback to the fishing trips provided a much-needed break from her work-related panic attack, but Taylor was still stressing out about her new job and how she was going to work her new sales territory.

Then, again, one specific fishing trip came to mind.

༄༄༄

When she was in elementary school, her family used to take summer vacations down to the sugar-white beaches of the Gulf Coast. They would do the typical things that families do on a beach trip—play and body surf in the waves, make not-so-perfect-looking sand castles, hunt for shells and starfish along the beach in the early mornings and late evenings, and eat lots of fresh seafood and ice cream. Taylor and her dad would also get in at least one fishing adventure per trip to the beach.

This particular father-daughter excursion found the two fishing in the warm waters of a vast, pristine bay known for attracting a variety of gamefish. Pops had performed his usual prep work on the tackle, maps, and gear, and everything was ready to go. Their game plan also had an added edge to it. He had some inside knowledge of the part of the bay they would be fishing.

The morning after their family arrived at the beach (while everyone else was sleeping in after the long trip), he had chartered a guide for a half-day trip and fished a section of the bay with an expert who was highly recommended at the local tackle stores. The guide, Capt. Gary, was a life-long resident of this area and had fished these waters year-round in every possible weather condition for over forty years. He was a really nice guy who looked and sounded like what was expected— he had a wiry build and dark, tan skin that was rough and weathered from spending a lifetime in this coastal environment. He possessed a quick wit and an easy laugh. He had a smooth, calming Southern accent, but there was no question of who was in charge when he spoke. Capt. Gary knew these waters like the back of his hand and could catch fish blindfolded.

After Pops met Capt. Gary at the marina, they prepared to venture out into the water in a customized twenty-foot bay boat. Prior to leaving the dock, Capt. Gary provided some tips. He explained the importance of using a thin-diameter, light line. The thin line would allow the bait or lure to act freely and lively—the more action the bait produced, the more likely it was to attract fish. He also stressed the importance of using smaller than normal hooks for basically the same reason. Fortunately, Taylor's dad had prepared his gear in the same way because he liked to use his own tackle, but he could always use some of Capt. Gary's gear in a pinch.

The first place they stopped was in about six feet of water located over a large grass flat—a place where sea grass grew to around two to two-and-a-half-feet tall from the bottom of the bay. He explained to Taylor's dad that these types of areas held a large number of baitfish and shrimp—two of the favorite meals for speckled trout and redfish. This grass flat covered approximately three acres, and the plan was to use the morning breeze to silently push the boat over different parts of the flat and avoid spooking the fish with the sound of the motor. They were using scented, artificial baits that imitated and smelled like the natural forage. Capt. Gary used a shrimp imitation and Taylor's dad used something that resembled a small baitfish.

"Let's start throwing these and get on some fish," whispered Capt. Gary.

The two started making long casts and varying the speed of their retrieves. One would reel it in slowly and the other would use a faster retrieve. After ten minutes of making casts into the calm water, Capt. Gary hooked and landed a nice two-pound speckled trout.

"Throw over there where I got bit and see if they're going to be picky today," he said.

Taylor's dad made cast after cast without any luck.

"Here, switch baits and slow down your retrieve," Capt. Gary instructed.

Pops changed lures, tied on a scented shrimp imitation, made another cast, and began to slowly twitch his bait back to the boat. Boom! Another two-pound speck immediately slammed onto his lure. After a testy fight, the saltwater trout was hauled overboard and tossed into the cooler.

"Okay, they're going after the shrimp on a slow retrieve this morning. Let's fish around this area until the sun gets a little higher in about an hour or so," said Capt. Gary.

His coaching worked. Twelve fish later, they cranked up the motor and moved to a different part of the large bay where the Marine Resources Division of the Department of Natural Resources had put in an artificial reef through a cooperative agreement with the US Army Corps of Engineers. This particular reef was about the size of a football field and consisted of huge mounds of oyster shells submerged on the bottom of the bay.

"This oyster bed attracts a lot of bait and provides a good ambush place for the big fish. The big boys will hide on the down-current sides of the shell bar and let the tidal flow move the baitfish in their direction." Capt. Gary grinned. "The tide is still coming in, and we'll start on the south side of the bar and drift over it. The fish will typically face into the current, so we'll need to cast in this direction so our baits will swim with the current and look more natural. Keep a fairly tight line so your bait doesn't get hung on the oysters."

He also instructed Taylor's dad to tie on a three-foot piece of heavier line to his main line, and then attach his lure to that. "These shells have razor-sharp edges that will cut your line in a heartbeat. You'll lose a lot of bait without that leader," explained the seasoned guide.

He moved the boat to about a hundred feet up current from the reef and cut off the motor. "What are you waiting for? Start casting!" cracked Capt. Gary.

The south Alabama born-and-bred charter guide really knew what he was talking about. The pair made a total of four slow drifts over different parts of the shell bar, and the fish were extremely cooperative. They couldn't make more than a few casts without getting a bite. The teacher taught the student well and between them, the twosome caught and released seven more speckled trout, five ladyfish, one flounder, four decent-sized redfish, and one bonnethead shark before the tide came to a standstill.

It was almost noon, so they decided to wrap things up and head back to the marina. After they tied up the boat, Taylor's dad thanked Capt. Gary and paid him for his time.

"I enjoyed it! You're a good guy and I wish that all my customers were as eager to learn as you. I hope that we can fish together again, and feel free to take your little girl to any of the spots that I showed you today," said the captain. "Please call me on my cell phone if you ever have any questions. I'll help you in any way that I can."

"Wow, that would be great!" smiled Taylor's father. "I'll take all of the help that I can get. Thanks again."

Armed with this knowledge and a new infusion of confidence, he couldn't wait to take his little girl fishing!

The two then went their separate ways. Capt. Gary went back to clean his boat so that everything would be ready for his next charter, and Taylor's dad scooted back to the vacation rental house to see what his family was doing.

At daybreak on Wednesday morning, the two eased out of the marina in a boat he had rented and made their way to a nearby grass flat. It was the same area that he fished a couple of days ago.

"Okay, honey, you use this shrimp imitation, and I'll start throwing this. Let's see if they're going to be picky today," he said echoing the words of Capt. Gary.

On only her third cast, Taylor felt a pull and her line became tight. "Got one!" she squealed.

"Reel it in, kiddo. Let's see what you caught," he said excitedly.

Her rod bowed sharply and the line was peeling off of her reel. Whatever was on the end of her line was not happy! After a few minutes of a game of kid vs. fish tug-of-war, Taylor's dad grabbed a nice fourteen-inch speckled trout from the murky water and proudly held it in front of her.

"Great job, kiddo! Look at this monster!"

She playfully counted the number of spots on the side of this radiant silver-and-black fish and gawked at the sharp teeth on the inside of its yellow mouth. Taylor wasn't totally thrilled after touching and smelling the protective slime on the fish's body. "Yuck." She giggled.

This scene went on and on throughout the day. The homework paid off well, and their daddy-daughter trip looked a lot like the trip that Pops shared with Capt. Gary a couple of days ago. The two floated and fished over the same general areas that her dad visited earlier in the week, and they even found a couple of secret spots of their own. He showed her the same things that he was taught and had learned over the years, explained why they were and weren't catching anything at different points throughout the day, and, most importantly, taught her how she could have fun—and be successful—if she ever wanted to go fishing on her own (i.e. without Daddy) when she grew older.

One of the things Taylor learned was the hierarchy of the food chain that exists in the ocean. She had a front-row seat to this when she witnessed a four-foot shark appear out of absolutely nowhere and chomp down on a flounder she was fighting. When she finally hoisted the flounder into the boat, all that was left of the tasty fish were the lips and a perfect U-shaped bite mark on the remaining half of the body. Among other things, Taylor's dad learned, experienced, and actually felt the exact decibel level that a preteenage girl reaches when her hooked flounder is bit in half by a four-foot shark that appears out of nowhere. Wow!

Taylor suddenly knew the answer. She needed to prepare for business in the same way that her dad prepared for a fishing trip. This made perfect sense to her. "Dad packed everything we needed and put together a plan for where we were going to fish. He knew where the fish should be located and what should interest them. All that we had to do was get to the area, put our baits in front of the fish, and give them the opportunity to bite," she reflected.

Dressed in baggy sweatpants and a well-worn t-shirt that she picked up in college, Taylor gathered all of the things that she would need tomorrow.

"Laptop, phone, and car charger? Check."

"Product literature? Check."

"Sales portfolio? Check."

"Samples, business cards, and a couple of extra pens? Got them."

She had everything she would need, but not so much that anything would get in the way.

While she was in her initial sales training session, an overview of the company's customer relationship program was installed on her laptop. Like most CRM programs, it provided account information, historical market share and revenue figures, and meeting notes taken by the previous rep. She powered up her computer and opened the program that listed all of her accounts. After sorting the list by ZIP codes, Taylor figured out a travel plan that would maximize her time in front of customers and minimize the dead time spent on the road.

She now knew what areas she was going to "fish" throughout the day.

Taylor spent some time in the "notes" section of the software program and researched each account that she planned to see tomorrow. By doing this, she was able to see what had and had not been discussed on previous sales calls and possibly found the potential "hot buttons" to discuss with each customer.

"This is awesome." She smiled.

The information gave her a good idea of what interests and possible objections she might encounter. By taking the time to search and navigate through the CRM program, she was able to put together a list of questions to ask and not ask in her meetings. Of more immediate importance, it helped reduce her current panic attack because it gave her a clearer picture of what to expect when she had those initial face-to-face meetings.

In fishing lingo, she determined what "bait" to use and she could visualize the "fish" being attracted to her presentation.

While reviewing the notes, Taylor discovered something that could possibly provide her added access to some heavy hitters in her line of work. Her relationships with these people could either make or break her efforts. Since one of her goals was to increase the market share of the IV antibiotic manufactured by her company, she needed the doctors working in her territory to prescribe it more often to a specific type of patient. The previous sales rep noted that three of the biggest decision makers in her region made their hospital rounds early in the morning at a nearby medical center to check on their patients. Taylor was no dummy. She knew that this was huge information. If she could convince a few well-respected physicians to use her IV antibiotic on a minimum of one additional patient per week, her sales numbers would quickly increase, and her market share would rise dramatically. Throughout her life, one of Taylor's best qualities was her sincerity and the genuine interest that she showed in others. People often felt like old friends with her after only one conversation. She knew that if she could get just a few minutes to introduce herself and speak with them in a relaxed atmosphere, relationships and trust could form and it would benefit her professionally.

Taylor felt certain she had just located a *honey hole* where the big fish were located. She now knew exactly where she would start *fishing* tomorrow and would be *on the water* early.

The sweat had stopped, and her pulse rate was back down to normal. Taylor began to laugh as she sat on the floor in her new apartment. "I never imagined that the fishing trips with my dad would help me with my first real job." She chuckled.

As she packed all of her sales materials into her car, she caught herself thinking the phrase her dad had uttered countless times: "Better to have and not need than need and not have." She also laughed at the fact that she was about to drive to the gas station to fill up her car so that she would be ready to go early the next morning... just like her dad used to do.

"All I have to do now is eat a Pop-Tart on the way out tomorrow and it will be deja vu." She smiled to herself.

♪♪♪

Fishing is A LOT like selling. Both require many of the same attributes, such as a never-ending supply of optimism, a willingness to learn and try new techniques, an inner drive to succeed, and dogged persistence. Finding success at both activities requires taking deliberate action on obvious—but often ignored—fundamental tasks. When these "basics" are performed consistently and flawlessly, anglers and business professionals share the sweet satisfaction and huge sense of accomplishment when their targeted species is attracted to the offering, hooked, and landed.

Don't think that you are involved in the world of sales? Think again. Just because your "product" isn't manufactured, installed, applied, performed, boxed, or shipped doesn't eliminate you from involvement in the sales process. You don't have to have an official title or job description that includes the words "business development," "account executive," or "product consultant" to be involved in sales.

Accountants are selling their knowledge of the current tax laws and attention to detail. Physicians are selling their training and expertise. Customer service representatives are selling their ability to help. Television anchors are selling trust. Warehouse personnel are selling efficiency. Ministers and clergy are selling a path to inner peace, redemption, and salvation. Spouses are selling teamwork, unity, and unconditional love. **When viewed at the very basic level, every individual is selling their competency and reliability to perform their specific role—can they and will they do what they say they will do in the time frame that they said they will do it?**

Whether you are a seasoned business professional looking for ways to stay on top of your game, a person in the middle of a career change, or an individual making the initial jump into the professional working world, the key to success lies in your ability and desire to constantly learn, prepare, and perform focused activities that are consistent with your goals and the goals of your employer.

This book will provide simple, powerful tips on how you can "fish" your way to producing award-winning sales revenue, increased productivity, and time-saving improvements in efficiency—regardless of the product, service, or solution you are offering.

Do you want to learn how to minimize your nonproductive hours, increase your focus, and maximize your earning potential? If so, then read on.

CHAPTER 2
CHECK YOUR FLY

Todd was so excited that he couldn't sit still. He loves to go fly-fishing for trout in a gorgeous river that runs through the mountains about sixty miles away from where he lives. Due to the long hours required by his "real job" (he owns his own wealth management company), his time spent standing knee-deep and flinging a fly in the chilly waters of this particular stream have been on the decline in recent years. But he had cleared his schedule and was heading out for a full day on the water tomorrow.

As a way of unwinding from the daily demands of his profession, Todd would sneak away after dinner every now and then to the man cave in his basement and tinker with an assortment of small hooks, deer hair, exotic feathers, yarn, glue, scissors, and various spools of colored thread. This after-hours refuge had a complete fly-tying station built on a section of the workbench that ran alongside the wall in the back corner of his unfinished basement.

With an AM talk radio show barely audible in the background and his ten-year-old yellow Lab curled up at his feet, Todd escaped from the stress associated with customer demands and deadlines into a quiet world of creativity and craftsmanship. Time stood still in this slightly musty and dusty environment.

Peering through his reading glasses underneath the glow of fluorescent lighting, Todd would delicately cut, wind, and glue bits and pieces of the fly-tying material onto a tiny hook held firmly in the vise clamped to his workbench. The finished products would be miniature masterpieces that would hopefully be attractive to fish when fastened to the end of his line.

By the evening prior to this particular fishing trip, Todd had completed eight new flies to add to the assortment that he was going to use the next day. He put them alongside the others in his fly box, turned off the light and the radio, and went upstairs to get some sleep before the big day.

When morning came, it did not arrive in glorious splendor. Todd's alarm clock failed to go off and he had overslept. He went from a peaceful slumber to a hurried pace in a matter of seconds. Todd jumped out of bed, grabbed his gear in the garage, and scrambled to get out of the house as quickly as possible.

About twenty minutes after pulling out of his driveway, Todd looked down and noticed that he was nearly out of gas, so he had to stop and fill up. But when he pulled into the gas station, he realized that his wallet was sitting on his kitchen table at home.

That was okay. He always kept some cash hidden in the glove compartment and could use that for payment. He found his stash of emergency money—three $20 bills. He figured that should be enough to get him to the mountains and back home. Todd gassed up with the speed of a NASCAR pit crew and was on his way.

When he arrived at his normal "put-in" spot, Todd pulled off the narrow road and parked his truck next to one of the large trees located a few yards off the shoulder so it would be in the shade and out of the way of the periodic traffic moving up and down the winding road.

Even though he was running a couple of hours later than expected, he was still excited about the possibilities that lie swimming in the river just a few yards away from him.

Quickly, he jumped out of his truck, grabbed his fly rod and his vest, and headed to the edge of the stream. Then it hit him. He had forgotten his waders!

"Dang it!" blurted Todd. "Okay, this isn't going to kill my day off," he told himself.

Todd figured that he had three choices—make the hour-long trip back to his house and get his waders, go to a nearby Wal-Mart and buy a new pair, or just fish without them. He was already running late so he didn't want to drive all the way back home and burn up another two hours. The water was too cold to stand in it in just his shorts, so he decided to make the fifteen-minute drive to the local Wal-Mart and purchase a new pair of waders.

When he pulled into the parking lot and parked his truck, Todd walked with purpose to the sporting goods section and found a pair of waders that would hopefully fit him. He took them to the checkout counter and when the nice lady rang up the sale, Todd remembered again that his wallet was sitting on the kitchen table at home.

"Daaaaaaang it!" he forcefully blurted again.

Todd's face began to turn an embarrassed shade of red and his temper was getting hot. But he was smart enough to know that he could only be mad at himself.

After a quick "breathe in/breathe out" session standing in line at the world's largest retailer in a small town located exactly in the middle of nowhere, he decided that he'd just suck it up and tough it out. He was going to go fishing, even if it meant immersing his bare legs in that chilly water.

He stomped out of the store empty-handed.

Fortunately, it didn't take him long to make it back to his parking place at his spot next to the river. He parked his truck, grabbed his gear, and weaved his way down the bank, carefully avoiding the poison ivy that crept onto the small path. When he reached into his vest pocket to grab one of his handcrafted masterpieces to tie on the end of his line, Todd was hit with the rude realization that he had left his fly box on the workbench in his basement.

"You've got to be kidding!" he said to himself.

Thankfully, he remembered that he had hooked an old, rusty fly to the outside of the driver's-side visor in his truck—he put it there so he would see it as he drove to and from work as a reminder of the old "all work and no play . . ." saying. It would have to do.

After he trudged to and from his truck and tied his one and only fly to his line, Todd gingerly took a step in the water.

"Whewwwww, that's cold!" he yelled without realizing it.

He took another few steps until he was around ten yards away from the bank. Finally, the fishing trip that he had anxiously waited for was finally underway.

Just upstream a few hundred yards away from him, the water took a wide swing around a large boulder before straightening out to flow over the shallow shoals where he was now standing. This elbow in the river was an area below some fairly small but swift rapids. Behind the boulder where the current slowed, the water formed a large, deep pool about four to five feet in depth. As Todd shuffled close to that part of the river, he noticed some dark shadows slowly moving around. They would come to the surface and then disappear back into the greenish-blueish depths. It appeared that the shadows were swimming to the surface and kissing the top of the water.

Todd immediately recognized that these shadows were actually hungry trout, and they were feeding on insects as they floated downstream. With the elegance of an orchestra conductor, he rhythmically swept his line back and forth overhead and cast his rusty fly a few feet above the area where he'd seen the shadows in the water. A few seconds after his furry little lure drifted slowly along the edge of the pool, one of those shadows swam up and engulfed his offering.

"One cast made. One rainbow trout caught. Not bad!" he triumphantly stated after netting the brilliantly colored fish.

Todd would focus in this area the remainder of the day, and he had figured out a good way to manage the cold water-induced pain. He would fish for about fifteen or twenty minutes until he could no longer stand the frigid flow. Then he would wade back to the bank or step out of the river onto the boulder and warm up until he could feel his legs and feet coming back to life. When his teeth stopped chattering and his legs were no longer the nice whitish-purplish-pinkish color brought on by the cold water, he would wade back into the river and fish some more.

After repeating this routine a number of times, Todd decided to call it a day. He had enough. He caught a respectable total of five trout, but his legs and feet were absolutely numb.

As he shuffled his way out of the cold water and stiffly walked back to his truck, he noticed a large, muscular man dressed in green pants and a khaki shirt standing nearby. That color-coordinated outfit draped over a large, muscular man standing in or near the woods usually meant one thing; and in this instance, it held true. It was Mr. Game Warden and he wanted to talk.

"I noticed that you had some luck with the trout today," the warden said. "Way to go, sir! Do you mind if I take a peek at your fishing license?"

That was the last thing Todd needed to hear. He was whipped. "You've got to be kidding," he mumbled under his breath. He was wet, cold, muddy, and hungry and had actually fished on his only day off from work in ready recollection for a whopping total of two hours. Now the game warden wanted to see his license, which was sixty miles away in his wallet on the kitchen table at home.

Through gritted teeth, he slowly explained the entire situation to the game warden—from oversleeping, forgetting his waders, making the trip to Wal-Mart, to leaving his wallet and fly box at home.

"It sounds like you've really had a day. I'm sorry, sir, but I'm going to have to issue you a citation for fishing without a license," explained the warden. "Rules are rules. Maybe next time, you'll take some time to prepare before you head up this way," the officer lectured.

〽️

Does Todd's eventful fishing trip remotely resemble anything that you've faced in a professional situation?

Meet Dan. Dan is a young go-getter in his mid-twenties. He had a number of job opportunities after graduating from college but chose to join his father's company in the financial services industry. Dan is Todd's son.

He began his professional career by answering the phone, preparing information packets, and generally doing whatever he could to help around the office to gain industry knowledge. No task was too small or too large.

After two years of learning the ropes inside the confines of the office, Dan began to make sales calls on businesses in the area. Through the connection of a friend, he was able to build some relationships inside of the largest employer in town and schedule a meeting with all of the top executives and decision makers. This appointment happened after months of conversations, casual meetings, and lunches with company insiders and was a result of the trust that had been built along the way.

Dan's expectations were sky-high, and he could see himself performing well in front of this group.

His objective was to present the various retirement services and products that his company provided and to gain an agreement to administer and manage the prospect's 401k packages. If the presentation went well and the decision was made to move forward, the sudden flood of resulting revenue would completely change Dan's (and Todd's) standard of living.

The week prior to his meeting was extremely hectic. The phones were ringing off of the hook, he had to attend a number of unscheduled meetings, and his inbox was bombarded with e-mails and customer requests. He had been pulled in a thousand different directions at work on the days leading up to his presentation, but it was finally "go-time" at 9:00 the next morning.

Things seemed to be running smoothly as he was being escorted into the conference room. Dan looked good, felt good, and sounded good. He was charming. After he found his place at the head of the table and began to make small talk with the executive team, he noticed that everyone was sitting alertly and hanging intently on his every word. *I have them in the palm of my hand*, he thought.

As Dan transitioned from the small talk and began to get down to business, he gracefully stood and booted up his laptop to begin his PowerPoint presentation. While progressing through the first part of the presentation, he—and everyone else in the room—realized that the changes he made last week weren't saved, the slides were out of order, and the name of the prospect's organization was badly misspelled.

Dan was visibly rattled, and the presentation went straight downhill at a rapid pace. All of the goodwill and positive feelings were sucked out of the room due to the sloppiness of the presentation. Dan desperately tried to regain control of the situation. He stuttered and stammered and tried his best to tap dance around the mistakes, but nobody was paying him any attention. He could even detect a few snickers directed toward him from the conversations that were now taking place. The meeting ended with an embarrassed and uncomfortable "thank you for sharing you time with me today."

He blew it.

It was no surprise to Dan when he learned the following day that the decision makers in the room chose to go with another company to administer their retirement packages. "If you don't take the time to prepare for a simple forty-five-minute presentation, then why in the world should we believe that you will pay any attention to our retirement savings?" he was bluntly told.

Had Dan taken an extra minute or two the night before his big meeting to make sure that everything was ready to go, then the outcome would probably have been different.

The most common thread between Todd's fishing trip, Dan's meeting, and a day-in-the-life of a business professional is the unfortunate waste of time and missteps caused by a combination of rushing through the day and a lack of proper planning. *Too often, people get caught in the exhausting trap of **being busy** and lose focus on their main objective.* They operate in a defensive mode reacting to each and every event, instead of taking the time to prioritize and work each day by taking intentional action on achieving their goals.

Individuals operating in a defensive or reactive mind-set often turn into "desk jockeys" that are constantly stuck at their desk reading and responding to e-mails. They get corralled to attend unscheduled meetings that don't fully apply to their area of expertise because they didn't have anything else planned. People with a reactive mind-set are the ones who get sucked into time-killing, nonrevenue-producing activities that disrupt and delay any *offensive* efforts that could lead to business growth.

How do you stay on offense? Plan, prioritize, and consciously manage how you spend your working hours.

While it's not some newly discovered, earth-shattering breakthrough in human performance, the simple activity of listing and ranking your priorities prior to each day, checking them off upon completion, and ending your day by reviewing, listing, and prioritizing your goals for the following day will work wonders for your productivity and keep you focused. The power comes from actually listing your priorities in writing—either on paper or on a dry-erase board—and managing that list throughout the day. Think of each goal as the final destination of a planned fishing trip (i.e. Todd's put-in spot next to the river) and each associated task as a landmark along the way. As you cross off each task upon completion, you will have a visual map of your path to success. When you review the list at the end of each day, it will show a clear picture of how much progress was made on your journey and what "landmarks" you will need to pass in the coming days to reach your destination.

Are you traveling straight to your destination or are you making some unnecessary stops and veering off on some side roads?

The game warden hit the nail on the head. **You need to take time to prepare so the next day will run smoothly.**

Plan your day. Every day.

Stay focused on your main objective.

Make it a priority to consistently write down, prioritize, and manage the tasks needed to reach your goals and track your journey to success.

CHAPTER 3
THUMPIN' THE LID

Garrett and his family lived in a nice subdivision on the outskirts of a large metropolitan city. In the middle of this thirty-year-old cluster of houses was a sixteen-acre lake that was full of bass, bluegill, and some wily old catfish. In the summer, and after school, Garrett could be found roaming the bank of this lake doing his best to try and catch something.

He loved to fish. Garrett grew up fishing with his dad and uncle and really knew what he was doing. Even though he was only twelve, he possessed a good understanding of the "how, when, where, and why" that it took to catch fish. Garrett understood something that many adults don't—he knew that the small details could make a huge difference in catching versus not catching anything. For example, he realized that a trophy fish could come loose if his line was connected to his lure with a poorly tied knot. He wanted to be ready when he hooked a whopper, so he practiced tying various knots until he had mastered each one.

When he was not fishing in the neighborhood lake, he would often play a game of target practice in his backyard with his rod and reel. With a quarter-ounce weight tied to the end of his line, Garrett would make casts and try to hit a garbage can lid that he had put out on the lawn. When his weight hit the trash can lid, it made a distinctive *thump* that could be heard from the driveways and backyard decks in his section of the neighborhood. He would start out with the lid about ten yards away from him, cast, and try to hit the plastic lid with his weight. After he consistently thumped the lid at that distance, he would move farther away and try it again. This game continued until he ran out of real estate and/or daylight, or his dog became too much of a nuisance chasing his casts and trying to bite the weight.

Garrett studied hard in middle school and made above average grades, but he was also a student of fishing. He came from a long line of educators—Garrett's mom and grandparents were teachers—and the concepts of study and preparation had been ingrained in him since he was a toddler. He read, watched, and listened to anyone who had any angling knowledge, in an attempt to increase his skill set to use on any upcoming fishing adventures.

Even though his TV time was somewhat limited, Garrett watched as many fishing shows on television as his parents would allow and when he found time in between sports, doing his homework, or just being a kid. He witnessed the likes of Bill Dance, Roland Martin, and Jimmy Houston reel in the big ones and imagined himself doing the same whenever the opportunity arose. From the comfort of the TV room at his house, he would sit in the slightly out-of-date recliner and watch as those tried-and-true fishermen would explain "how to think like a fish." As a reflection of his television viewing habits, Garrett would wear the traditional Bill Dance white-and orange-baseball hat with the big "T" on the front, laugh like Jimmy Houston, and would always say a big "Oh, son!" when he hooked something . . . just like ole Roland.

Garrett was required to sell magazines as part of a fundraising contest for his school. Fortunately, he could always count on producing at least one customer with his sales efforts. Because of his persistent begging and his zeal for hooking anything that swims with scales, his parents would always purchase subscriptions to a couple of fishing magazines. Garrett couldn't wait for those to show up in the mailbox each month! He would scour each publication from cover to cover to find some new techniques to try and learn how the experts went about their business. Those publications were like textbooks for fishermen because they contained information on all aspects of angling—from choosing the right tackle, bait presentation, and how to "read" a lake to determine the productive areas to fish. He studied those magazines almost as much as he studied his school material.

When he couldn't actually go fishing, one of his favorite things to do was to visit the new Bass Pro Shops retail outlet that recently opened near his house and attend one of their seminars. At certain times each year, Bass Pro Shops hosts seminars in all of their store locations and gives the public a time to listen, learn, and ask questions to people who catch fish for a living. Garrett loved those seminars and was eager to rub shoulders with the pros. He understood that it was a special opportunity to learn from the best and would do everything possible to get his mom or dad to take him to these unique events.

Garrett would do just about anything to help himself become a better angler.

♪♪♪

A lot of professional sales executives and small business owners could learn a thing or two from this kid.

How many times have you met with a customer or prospect and realized that you should have taken more time to prepare in order to fully understand the subject matter that was being discussed?

Remember, you are the expert when talking about your product, service, or solution. You are the consultant, the mentor, and the coach who can provide the answer to a problem. Keep in mind that the client or prospect wouldn't have graciously shared his or her time with you if they already knew the specifics and value of your offering. You *must* have a solid foundation of knowledge about the subject matter. If you don't know what you're talking about, then you're wasting your time and the time of your prospect or customer.

Prepare yourself for anything that might be thrown your way during a meeting with a client or prospect. Educate yourself on your product(s), industry, and, if possible, your customer. **Know your business environment inside and out so that you ARE considered an expert and the most reliable go-to source for a solution.**

There will be times when you are not able to confidently answer a specific question. If you do not know a certain detail or are not sure if your response is 100 percent accurate, it's okay to acknowledge that reality. It is better to explain to your customer that you are not completely certain and will provide them with accurate information as quickly as possible once you verify your response. You will gain credibility by doing this and avoid losing trust if your initial answer is not true and accurate. You will also be ready if and when this question is asked again and can provide the answer with complete confidence.

Do your homework. Industry trade publications, webinars, books, and blogs are readily available and provide valuable information to those wanting to get an edge on their competition. However, the knowledge is not going to magically seep into your brain. You have to be willing to do some research and take the time to learn.

Practice makes perfect. The time that Garrett spent in the backyard honing his casting skills by "thumping" the trash can lid made him deadly accurate when he was fishing. He could cast his lure around stumps, under docks and overhanging branches, into the spots where the fish were hiding. As a result of the time he spent practicing, Garrett's muscle memory and hand-eye coordination were so highly developed that he could place his offering wherever he wanted by simply focusing on the target area, making the cast, and allowing the bait or lure to follow his line of sight. He rarely missed his target.

Sales executives and business development professionals need to practice "thumping" their presentations until they hit their target consistently and with silky-smooth ease.

Make it a top priority to rehearse the key communication points that explain how you and your solution provide value and solve specific problems for your customer. Tell the story. Present the "how" and the "why" your offering will help customers attain their goals.

Rehearse your presentation in front of someone (spouse, roommate, friend, dog, etc.) or some*thing*. **It is extremely important to know how you sound and understand how you present yourself.** Practice in front of a mirror or record yourself with your smartphone—you may think that you come across as genuine, confident, and believable but your body language, tone, and inflection may present an entirely different image.

Practice until you feel comfortable and the butterflies have gone away. Practice until the "uh's" have been eliminated. Practice until you *do* sound genuine, confident, and believable.

Imagine that you are the customer when listening or watching yourself. Ask yourself if you would buy something or do business with this person after hearing your sales pitch. Unless the answer is a definite yes, keep practicing!

It is perfectly natural to experience some nervousness the first few times you present your product or solution to a potential customer. Over time and with repetition, you will become more comfortable discussing the subject matter and feel more at ease when talking with a customer or prospect. Arm yourself with knowledge so that your confidence will show whether you're speaking face-to-face, over the phone, or leading a discussion in a group setting. **The key is to minimize the time it takes to feel totally comfortable with your subject**

matter. There is no secret or magic involved in this. It comes with practice.

Learn from a pro. The seminars at Bass Pro Shops are well attended because people want to hear how the top anglers in the world handle certain situations. They want to hear what works and what doesn't work. The audience wants instruction on how, when, and why these experts catch fish when others can't catch a thing. Those in attendance are there to improve their chances of finding success and willingly drive long distances to soak up the wisdom of the best and most accomplished in their sport.

The high-achieving business professional will also search for opportunities to gain wisdom from the best and most successful in their industry. **If you want to grow your business and increase your sales, then make it a top priority to learn from those who have achieved what you are trying to achieve.**

Search for sources that will feed your quest for success. **Find a mentor**—someone who has "been there, done that" and has achieved success—and build a trusting relationship with them.

Offer to take the #1 salesperson in your company to lunch and have an honest, open discussion on how you can get better. **People will go out of their way to help if you show humility and have a genuine interest in learning.**

Pay close attention to the small details. One little extra step in preparation can produce huge dividends and provide a smoother, straighter journey of the road to success.

Practice so that the trophy isn't lost when the opportunity arises.

CHAPTER 4

ELIMINATE THE DEAD WATER

What if an angler could see what was underneath the water? Would that help them locate and catch more fish? Most definitely. But for years, anglers had to rely on local knowledge or just hope that a fish would be in the general area as their bait.

Then came the breakthrough.

In 1959, a company by the name of Lowrance introduced a product that totally changed the sport of fishing. They introduced the public to an easy-to-use version of sonar that was based on the technology developed and used by the US Navy during World War II. This product had four basic components: a transmitter that produces an electrical impulse, a transducer that converts the impulse to a sound wave that is sent down in the water, a receiver, and a display. Simply explained, the transmitter and transducer work together to send and receive sound waves underneath the water. When the sound waves detect a solid mass below the surface, they echo and bounce back to the receiver. That information is converted into electronic signals and sent to a display screen in the form of different colored bars and blips. By interpreting the information on the screen, fishermen could now understand what was below the boat.

People could now see if there were fish underneath them.

This technology provided a way to view the bottom of a lake, ocean, or river. Anglers could now pinpoint the changes in water depth and the location of bottom irregularities. They could detect the exact location of channel boundaries, reefs, stumps, brush, and rock piles. Most importantly, this product showed where the fish were located. (Flash forward to today and the technology has evolved to where anglers can now witness a 360-degree

ELIMINATE THE DEAD WATER

view of whatever is occurring beneath the water and see bottom contour in three-dimensional pictures!)

Many believe that nobody uses this technology as proficiently as professional bass anglers. Why? Because it saves them time and helps them make money—the tournament angler who catches the heaviest limit of fish cashes the biggest check and wins the largest prizes. Studies have shown that 90 percent of the fish are located in approximately 10 percent of the water in freshwater lakes and streams. By utilizing this technology, bass pros can concentrate their efforts on the "fishy" water and eliminate the low-potential areas. Fish can't be caught if they're not there.

In recent years, the Bassmaster Classic—the most prestigious tournament for professional freshwater anglers—was held on a large, deep-water impoundment that offered a variety of areas for the contestants to choose from and decide where they should focus their efforts. The anglers could fish any part of the lake, and their choices would ultimately determine their final standing in the event.

Would the bass be found near the bank? Would keeper-sized fish be found up the creeks or in the submerged timber? Are they congregating in shallow or deep water?

One hard-working professional angler capitalized on the new side-imaging technology and used it to help him win this million-dollar event.

In the weeks leading up to the Classic, he spent many days pre-fishing this lake with the intention of gaining an edge on his fellow competitors. As a result of his time spent studying the information produced by his side-imaging unit, he located one very small area that looked extremely promising. Out in the middle of the main body of the lake, approximately a mile from the dam, he discovered one irregularity on the bottom that was different than the surrounding lake floor. The bottom contour on this section of water was fairly flat and noneventful except for a pile of rocks that was about the size of three Chevy Suburban's parked side by side. The tournament angler knew that predator fish and baitfish would be drawn to this area because it provided shade, a break in the current, and a place to hide. Compared to the surrounding underwater terrain, this one relatively small spot stood out like a zit on a supermodel. It screamed, "This is where the fish are!" but the rock pile couldn't be detected from the surface or the bank. This area just looked like a big body of boring water.

There was no way that he could have found this unique fish attractor if he hadn't invested hours and hours of time using this new technology.

During the tournament, most of the anglers spent their time fishing in multiple areas of this reservoir. They would work in one area and maybe catch a fish or two, crank up their flashy, sponsor-branded bass boats and motor over to another location. The majority of the field would repeat this pattern until it was time to go back to the weighing station and check-in their catches to determine their standings in the tournament.

Each day, while the majority of the pros were churning up the water going up and down the lake in search of their prey, this one boat would consistently be found out in the middle of the main body of the impoundment. From a distance, it looked like this one contestant had either broken down and was experiencing engine problems, or he was just taking a break from the action.

He wasn't.

This professional angler had entered the GPS coordinates of the hidden rock pile into his navigation system when he was pre-fishing the lake, and his system directed him back to that exact location. Based on his time spent prepping and practicing, he knew that keeper-sized bass would be at that spot in full-out feeding mode at certain times of the day when the Corps of Engineers discharged water from the dam, causing an increase in current flow. The baitfish and predator fish "turned on" when the water was moving.

He spent almost 100 percent of his time during this grueling tournament fishing in this one location, and that decision proved to be the right choice. He caught the heaviest total of fish and won the tournament in decisive fashion.

Cha-ching! His professional life soared to new heights because he embraced the latest technology and combined it with his hammer-strong work ethic and meticulous preparation.

The sport of fishing has seen many advances since the days of cane poles, heavy braided line, cork bobbers, and a hook baited with a long, slimy night crawler. In addition to side-imaging sonar, the tackle and equipment

ELIMINATE THE DEAD WATER

has also improved dramatically. Super strong, sensitive, lightweight rods and reels made with hi-tech materials are now readily available and the norm. Sporting goods stores are now stocked with aisles full of laser-sharpened hooks, thin diameter thermo-fused lines that are strong and resistant to abrasions, and highly durable scented baits made of synthetic materials that look, feel, and smell like the "real thing."

Don't get me wrong. People can still catch fish using the same tackle and techniques that were used back in the early 1900s, but they're not giving themselves the best opportunity to succeed by using that type of antique equipment.

The same concept applies to selling. Professional salespeople can still close a deal by using old methods of preparation and techniques. But they're not putting themselves in the best position to win by clinging to the past.

If someone wants to keep their account data on 3" x 5" cards stacked and bound by a rubber band, that's their choice. If the primary activity of the person responsible for producing increased sales revenue is sitting at his or her desk waiting for a customer to call, then so be it. Unless that person is working for the company that has discovered and patented the cure for cancer or the common cold, then that tactic will not provide consistent business growth.

Sales representatives, managers, and business executives can still operate by fax, flip phones, and handwritten weekly reports if they'd like. Nontargeted "spray and pray" sales and marketing activities can work in certain environments, but it may be more effective and cost-efficient to use a targeted approach. "Old school" methods might work in a specific application, but there is a huge difference between "old school" and being behind the times.

Become familiar and comfortable with the most current technology designed to help you and your company operate in the most efficient way. For example, Customer Relationship Management (CRM) programs allow organizations to gather and interpret data on their current customer base, prospect lists, and marketing and sales activities. Even though CRM programs have been around for a while and are not exactly the newest technology, a surprising number of mid- to large-sized organizations have not invested in this type of tool to help increase their market share.

A common business saying is: "He or she who owns the data wins." That's very true. However, individuals and companies shouldn't collect data for the sake of collecting data or allow the excitement of a new program distract their focus away from the needs of the customer. Be careful and not let a tool designed to increase efficiencies become larger than the primary goal at hand—growing the business. If the goal is to gain sales revenue, then the more accurate saying should be: "He or she who owns, interprets, and acts upon the applicable data wins."

Nothing beats face-to-face, interpersonal communication with a customer or prospect. But you can't physically be in different places at the same time. **Multiply your "you."** Use e-mail blasts, texts, tweets, and webinars to communicate with your colleagues and clients to give them a consistent "touch" when you can't physically be in front of them. Just as top-producing anglers use technology to eliminate unproductive areas and locate potentially productive areas where fish can be caught, winning salespeople and organizations use technology to eliminate unproductive areas and locate markets, industries, and individuals that can possibly say yes to their offering.

Salespeople don't have to be hard-core techno geeks, but the high achievers are always on the lookout for tools that will streamline their efforts and maximize their productivity.

Unfortunately, some individuals and organizations adhere to the "this is the way that we do it, and will always do it" mind-set. "It's worked for us for (fill in the blank) years, so there's no reason to change now."

Uh huh. Don't use the outhouse when indoor plumbing is available.

Embrace technology. Use it to your advantage.

Fish where the fish are located.

CHAPTER 5
MATCH THE HATCH

Those passionate people who enjoy the artistry and tradition of using simplistic reels, sinking or floating lines, long wispy rods, and hand-tied flies live by the words "match the hatch." This phrase is the first commandment of fly-fishing.

While most types of fish can be caught on fly-fishing tackle, probably the most sought-after group is the various species of trout found throughout the country. These finicky fish are often found in beautiful, remote streams and rivers, and one of their main sources of food is insects.

The life cycle of an insect can be broken down and viewed in three stages—the reproductive formation of the eggs, their development into larvae, and when the larvae "hatches" and turns into the actual adult insect. Insect hatches occur at different times of the year.

Fly fishermen understand that their chances for success are the greatest when their offering most closely resembles the size, shape, and color of the current diet of the trout. Thus, match the hatch.

As mentioned in an earlier chapter, Todd was able to entice some rainbow trout to munch down on his offering. He was fortunate that his one-and-only fly was the exact color, size, and shape of the tiny bugs that the fish were feasting on in the chilly water. Although he didn't plan it that way, Todd's ability to match the hatch provided a much-needed glimmer of success to a mostly miserable day.

"Match the hatch" doesn't only to apply to fly fishermen. It's the universal concept to all of sport fishing—determine what the fish are eating and use whatever most closely resembles their current diet. If you are trying to catch smallmouth bass and discover that they are primarily feeding on four-inch crawfish, then you should use something that imitates a four-inch crawfish. If you want to catch striped bass and see that their main food source is blueback herring approximately five inches in size, then, guess what? You need to use something that closely resembles a five-inch blueback herring. It's not that hard to understand.

〽️

The same concept is true in professional selling. Determine the wants and needs of your customer and present your solution in a way and in the environment that's most attractive to them.

Match the hatch.

How do you discover the needs of your customers or prospects? Ask them.

Once the sales executive has a clear understanding of how they can assist, then he or she needs to present the solution in a way that's most attractive to the customer's personality type and in a way that matches their preferred method of communication. For example, some people prefer an abundance of information, technical data, and studies presented in a formal manner. They tend to arrive at conclusions based on data and facts. Others interpret and respond to situations based on emotion. These individuals respond well when asked, "How does that make you feel?" or "What are your feelings about that?"

Some individuals want to hear all of the background information and intricate details about the subject.

Others want the information presented in short, concise bullet points. These people want the highlights of the perceived problem and how you can solve that problem. Short and sweet.

Some customers communicate only through e-mails and texts.

Some want to chitchat over a meal.

Certain people prefer formal presentations conducted in conference room settings. Others would rather meet over coffee and trade ideas on the back of a paper napkin.

How do you find this information about your customer or prospect? Ask, listen, and observe during your next meeting with them and it will be fairly obvious how they prefer to operate in a business situation.

Practice different ways of presenting your solution so that you're prepared for any situation, whether it's a sixty-second "elevator speech" or an in-depth discussion conducted in a formal environment.

Regardless of the personality type of the customer, top-producing salespeople always ask more than they tell.

"What exactly would make your life easier?"

"What causes you the biggest headaches?"

"What did you have in mind?"

"How can I help make you the hero?"

"What are your goals for this quarter/year?"

"How can I help?"

"What would be your ideal solution?"

Etc.

By asking a number of valid questions, the successful salesperson is able to guide the prospect or customer and keep things on track. It helps the business development executive stay in tune with the needs of the customer and avoid spending time on features that provide no benefit.

The initial meeting should not be an interrogation of the customer or prospect. The best scenario is just a normal discussion that flows smoothly along. Ask questions that are appropriate to the situation and don't force them on your client. Remember, you are trying to help the customer. Smile. Slow down. Breathe. Imagine that you are talking to a friend. You're still trying to make a great impression, but the nervousness of a "first date" is nowhere to be found. Always try to bring the conversation back to the ultimate solution—**how your offering will help them meet their needs and help make their life easier.**

Ask valid questions, and then shut up and listen. There's an old saying that will forever ring true: "God made you with two ears and one mouth on purpose. You should listen twice as much as you speak."

Successful anglers understand how to "listen" to the fish by interpreting the fish's reaction or nonresponse to their offering. Do the fish bite on a slow or fast retrieve? Are they attracted to a small lure or a large lure? Do you detect more strikes from a bait that crawls along the bottom or one that swims erratically through the water column?

Customers are just like fish. They will tell you what they want if you simply observe and listen to what they are saying.

CHAPTER 6
TIME AND TIDE WAIT FOR NO MAN

Sally's dad, Bob, was an extremely successful businessman. He founded and presided over a regional building supply company that was forged with the simple ingredients of honesty and hard work. He invested many long hours in his company and went out of his way to bless his employees and customers. Bob's business philosophy was: "Listen and respond to the customers' needs and perform to the best of your ability."

Like most successful organizations, his company held regularly scheduled meetings where he and his managers met with the sales team and discussed opportunities, activities, their competition, and the general business environment. These topics are typical of any internal sales discussions held in any industry. The one item that made his sales meetings unique and memorable to the participants was that they were held each Friday morning promptly at 6:00.

Bob was a stickler about time management, especially when it came to internal meetings. Get in. Get out. Get to work. He felt that his team should meet when there were no distractions and at a time when all employees could attend. No phone calls. No traffic delays. No ball games, doctor's appointments, or dance recitals to attend. No excuses. Thus, they met promptly at 6:00 a.m.

"Time and tide wait for no man," Bob would always say.

Even though his business activities consumed the majority of each day, he always made time for his wife, children, and extended family. As a by-product of his success, Bob was able to purchase a nice place on the coast where he and his family could go and spend some quality time together.

This coastal property was a place of escape. Bob's family members could almost feel their blood pressure drop and the stress leave their bodies once they were out of the city limits and on their way to this little slice of heaven. The trip there took them on some winding, two-lane backroads through small "one red light" towns into a world of sandy soil, salty air, and thick humidity that seemed to ooze from the marshes and engulf your entire body like being gently wrapped in a warm, steamy washcloth.

This coastal property was also home base for Bob's passion outside of work—fishing.

When catching fish was at the top of the to-do list, this was not the ideal place to catch up on sleep. Just like at work, Bob liked to start early and extend the day.

"Whoever's going fishing . . . it's time to get up!" Bob would yell in the pre-dawn hours as he roused his sons, daughter, and son-in-law out of bed. "Time and tide wait for no man!"

Proper etiquette stated that Bob called the shots concerning the angling excursions, and you gladly did things his way. Two things were consistent on every trip—the day began before the sun was up and there was a heightened sense of purpose to entice something to bite your bait, hook, catch, and keep the regulation-sized fish in the cooler.

The house rules were "no catch/no eat" and the general understanding was that the main course for dinner each night would be a broiled, grilled, or fried concoction of what was caught earlier in the day. Bob and his family would either find themselves feasting on the catch of the day or sitting around the table nibbling on saltine crackers and boiled shrimp—if there were any leftover shrimp that weren't used for bait earlier in the day.

At the beginning of each day as their boat eased through the mist hovering over the salty marsh, Bob would ask, "Are we going to catch anything today?"

If the responses were along the lines of "I'm going to try" or "We sure hope so," Bob would ask the question again and again until he heard the correct answers: "Yes!" "Definitely!" "We're going to tear it up!"

"Now that's what I'm talking about!" Bob would say as he grinned from ear to ear. "Let's go catch some fish."

TIME AND TIDE WAIT FOR NO MAN

Bob fished in all types of weather conditions—good, bad, rainy, hot, and cold. "The fish are still in the water. They're not going to leave just because it's not perfect out there," he would say. "Let's go. Time and tide wait for no man."

~ ~ ~

Bob's rules provided focus and energy. Whether his crew ate well at night was largely determined by the decisions made in the boat based on the current conditions, their efficiency, and the fact that everyone was highly motivated to catch something. They didn't want to starve.

The same principles apply to the business world. Those who find success perform efficiently, effectively, and tirelessly. If it's necessary to complete a daily objective, they extend their productive hours on the job by starting early and finishing late. High achievers don't watch the clock; they're focused on the result.

Those superstars who consistently win at work put themselves in a positive frame of mind and maintain that positive outlook throughout the day.

Top-earning salespeople are competitive. They challenge themselves to reach new levels and strive to be listed as #1 on the internal sales rankings. They want to be viewed as leaders and to be publicly recognized at company meetings.

There is a sense of urgency for those climbing to new levels. Regardless of what's going on around them—good economy, bad economy, workplace drama, etc.—the top producers block out the noise, remain focused on the desired result, and work persistently to achieve their goals.

When Bob and his family visited their coastal property, the house rules were "no catch/no eat." The mind-set should be the same for sales professionals: "no sell/no eat."

Make the most out of the time spent in your professional life. Don't get distracted. Use your working hours wisely. *Focus your energy on activities that are in-line with the goals you have set.*

Each day is comprised of twenty-four hours. During those twenty-four hours, we sleep, eat, work, tend to family matters, and hopefully get to indulge in some free time. Each day begins anew regardless of how much was accomplished during the previous twenty-four-hour cycle. The clock keeps ticking and does not rewind. Once the day is over, you cannot get it back. The oceans will always ebb and flow, and the waves will keep coming ashore regardless of our presence here on Earth.

Time and tide wait for no man.

CHAPTER 7
THE MEN OF 1000 CASTS

Brian and Ron are rising stars in the world of professional tournament fishing.

The two initially met and became close friends in college, where they were members of the same fraternity. Among their peers, they didn't necessarily stand out as the tallest, shortest, smartest, loudest, or wildest, but they were definitely the most competitive pair of the bunch. Brian and Ron would compete at almost anything—high-class contests of who could eat the fastest, do the most pushups, burp the loudest, or stay awake the longest. Their one-on-one games of basketball held in the parking lot in front of the fraternity house on the goal with the bent rim and tattered net were things of legend. But the most heated competition occurred in the classroom.

Brian and Ron rarely took the same classes and were involved in different courses of study, but they each wanted to out-do the other in terms of bottom-line results. Their weekdays were filled with a large volume of good-natured trash talking ("You bombed that test, right?"; "There's no way that a guy with your IQ can make above a C in that class"; "You call sitting in front of the TV with a book in your lap, studying?", etc.). Then, on each Friday afternoon, they would compare their grades and record the results on a chart that Brian had printed and placed on the refrigerator in his room.

At the end of each semester when the final grades were posted, the person with the highest GPA won bragging rights and the most coveted "trophy" in the fraternity—the custodial services of the runner-up. More often than not, those cleaning efforts were specifically performed on the not-so-spotless and somewhat fuzzy domain of the bathroom. Both guys had a great inner drive to succeed and were highly self-motivated, but the thought of cleaning the others' nasty shower and commode provided a maximum-strength dose of incentive to grind it out in their studies.

One thing that Brian and Ron discovered during their freshman year was that they both shared a love for fishing. Brian was a full-blooded Cajun and grew up fishing in the bays and bayous near his parent's house in Louisiana. Ron spent countless hours catching bass, bream, and catfish in the lake on his grandparent's property, and both young men would "recharge their batteries" by wetting a hook when they had a break from college.

During the time they were obtaining their degrees, bass clubs were forming on numerous campuses, and tournaments began to spring up around the country specifically targeted toward the collegiate angler. The entry fees were affordable, the tournaments were held on weekends, and the majority of the competitions took place on lakes within easy driving distance from most college campuses. The only requirements were that the participants pay their fees, be actively enrolled in college-level classes, and considered to be in good standing at their places of higher learning.

When Brian and Ron heard that their university was starting a bass club, they jumped all over it! They became active members, and the young duo enjoyed the camaraderie and the chance to compete. By the time they graduated from school, their two-man team had fished in a total of six tournaments—they won two and finished in second place in the other four.

They worked well together as a team.

Ron like to fish deep. Brian liked to coax shallow-water fish into biting. The key ingredient to their success was that they both liked to fish *fast*. They figured that the best way to win a tournament was to always have a lure in the water. From the beginning of each tournament to the end, they agreed to make as many potentially productive casts as humanly possible and cover as much "fishy" water as time allowed.

The way that Brian and Ron viewed the situation, they figured that they could only catch something if their lines were wet. They understood the chances of catching fish directly correlated with the amount of time that their baits were in the fish's environment. They realized the odds of catching a limit of fish improved if they maximized the number of opportunities that they gave the fish to bite down on their baits. In addition, the quicker they caught their limit, the sooner they could "cull" their catch and replace the smaller fish with any larger, heavier fish that were caught.

The two used this basic philosophy to succeed in their collegiate tournaments and continued to use the strategy as they fished professionally on the bass and redfish tournament trails upon graduation.

༄༄༄

Those in the business of growing sales revenue must also understand that there is a direct link between product growth and the number of times that their product or solution is discussed with decision makers.

It's a numbers game.

The more times you have a *meaningful* discussion about your offering with a prospect or customer, the greater your chances are of achieving a positive outcome with that customer or prospect.

Regardless of your industry—insurance, multilevel marketing, financial, manufacturing, pest control, health care, custodial, industrial, automotive, high tech, low tech, white collar, blue collar, nonprofit and for-profit fundraising, etc.—your chances of succeeding increase tremendously the more times you interface with a customer or prospect.

This doesn't mean that you can increase your success rate by stopping by every other day and chitchatting with the receptionist of a potential client. Likewise, increased sales revenue won't suddenly appear on the monthly reports because your prospect's front office staff lets you take them out to lunch on Fridays. However, **your path to success will become shorter and straighter if you increase the number of discussions you conduct with qualified individuals and decision makers.**

Sales cycles can be joyously short or painfully long depending on many factors, such as the product, budget, industry, and size of the customer. An agreement can be made as a result of the initial meeting, or it can drag on for years of phone conversations, e-mails, lunches, and presentations. A key ingredient in all sales cycles is focused, positive communication with the person or group of individuals that have the authority to say yes and take action on the proposal. Keep the dialogue moving forward, but don't cross the line that separates you from being persistent to becoming a pest. A good follow-up e-mail or phone call is necessary but not appreciated if done too often.

THE MEN OF 1000 CASTS

If Brian or Ron was fortunate enough to locate an individual or school of fish, they understood that the fish can be spooked and swim away if they detected something out of the ordinary. Once they determined that fish were in the area, the two would try different techniques, baits, and presentations until they found the right combination that attracted a bite.

They often used one particular technique, *finesse fishing*, when conditions were extremely difficult and the fish just wouldn't bite. Finesse fishing is when anglers simply downsize their lures and tackle and s-l-o-w down their bait presentation, gently putting an offering in front of the fish. Brian and Ron learned that the subtle wiggle of a small bait often produced a strike when the fish wouldn't respond to larger, faster, and erratic presentations.

The same is true in business. Aggressively pursue new customers, but don't be scared to slow down and finesse your offering to avoid alienating your prospect.

Growing your customer base is challenging and competitive. If you don't receive the "yes" from the customer or prospect, someone else will. Your objective should be to get your offering or solution in front of more decision makers than those competing with you for that yes answer.

Brian and Ron understood that bringing in the heaviest limit of fish and winning a tournament would only happen if their lines were in the water and their lures were in front of their targets. The more opportunities they gave the fish to bite, the better their odds were of catching something.

Winning salespeople understand the same principle. **The more often their solution is presented, the better their odds are of selling something. Give people the opportunity to say yes.**

Don't spook the fish.
Make as many casts as you can.
Keep your line wet and your bait in front of the fish.

CHAPTER 8
DON'T BE A POSER

Doug lived on the western coast of central Florida near Tampa. He had finally built enough solid customer relationships and had trained his assistant to manage his business affairs so that he could now slip away from work a few hours early on some days and go fishing. Professionally, he was still in accumulation mode and was actively focused on building his customer base. But he had reached a very comfortable level of income and being away from the office for a few hours every now and then wasn't going to kill him.

Doug was an impeccably dressed man, whether in a professional or casual setting. His pants were always sharply creased, his shirts always neatly pressed, and he had "the look" of a successful businessman who just walked out of a lunch meeting at an exclusive country club. Heck, he even smelled good.

His fishing attire was much the same. Doug wore only button-down, collared shirts and multipocketed shorts made of the latest generation of moisture-wicking fabrics. Perched on top of his head was a spotless, bright visor bearing the logo of the latest "hot" engine, boat, or lure manufacturer. He covered his eyes with a $250 pair of polarized sunglasses or let the expensive shades hang around his neck on a titanium lanyard. Doug went all out to present himself as a serious angler.

He had recently purchased a new boat, and it was s-w-e-e-t! He bought an eighteen-foot center-console flats boat complete with a thirty-gallon livewell, an elevated poling platform, mounted electronics, Power-Pole shallow-water anchor, and a shiny 115-horsepower outboard engine.

His fishing tackle consisted of multiple combinations of expensive carbon fiber rods and highly engineered, corrosion-resistant reels. Doug had a massive collection of artificial lures that were neatly organized in labeled storage containers and arranged by their shape, size, color, and fishing application.

DON'T BE A POSER

It seemed like everyone in Tampa's fishing world knew this man. He was greeted with a hearty "Doug!" when he walked into any of the local marinas or tackle stores. It reminded you of the greeting that the character Norm received on the popular 1980s-era television show Cheers.

All of the charter guides knew Doug on a first-name basis, and he could talk fishing with the best of them.

Doug's problem was that he hardly ever caught any fish. He never caught much of anything, even though he lived minutes away from some of the best fishing waters in the world. He had all of the finest, most expensive equipment. Doug owned a custom-made boat that was ideal for the environment and conditions in that area. Through his relationships with the local charter guides, he possessed inside information on what, when, and where the fish were biting. And don't forget the high-dollar sunglasses and moisture-wicking outfits he wore.

What was the problem?

༄༄༄

Stacy worked hard. She was always the first to arrive at the office and the last person to leave. She spent so much time at work that the after-hours security guards and cleaning crew knew her on a first-name basis.

She was intelligent, fit, and smartly dressed.

Stacy worked for a software company and had the potential to earn a very enviable income if she could produce results for her employer. She graduated in the top of her class from a prestigious Ivy League university and earned an MBA from that same historic place of higher learning. (Just listen closely and you'll hear about her college degrees; she found a way to work it into every conversation.)

She prepared presentations on every software application offered by her company and spent many hours practicing and fine-tuning her delivery. Stacy was also proudly "paperless," keeping all of her notes, product, and account information on her laptop, tablet, and iPhone.

An enormous amount of her time was spent charting sales trends and projections and maintaining and growing her connections on LinkedIn. She blogged. Stacy was always at her desk typing and banging away at something on her keyboard.

On those rare occasions she would break away from her desk to stretch her legs, Stacy made a point of walking past the executive offices and saying hello to the company hierarchy.

She met regularly with the programmers and product directors and participated in webinars and conference calls with all of the regional offices scattered from coast to coast. Her plate was full. Stacy's work was her life.

Surprisingly, her sales stunk. Stacy's numbers were awful.

∫∫∫

Doug wanted to catch more fish. Stacy wanted to increase her sales. The two of them were thoroughly prepared, highly educated on their subject matter, and fully equipped for success, but neither was realizing their potential. If this were college or professional sports, then Doug and Stacy would be selected to the "All Airport" team—the big, strong athletic folks who looked great coming off of the airplane but couldn't play worth a flip.

Why weren't they successful?

Doug needed to know the "secret" to catching more fish. Stacy needed to know the "secret" to increasing her sales. This "secret" is the same for both situations, and it's not really a secret at all. It's easy to say and easy to do, but many people overlook the obvious. If they both incorporated this strategy into their endeavors, it would be impossible for them to not increase their rates of success.

Doug and Stacy needed to actually "do" the activity.

Not study it. Not chart it or graph it. And not talk about it with their peers. They needed to stop dancing around the activity and be deliberate about performing the activity, whether it was trying to catch fish or close a sale.

If Doug wanted to catch more fish, then he needed to go fishing! He needed to get on the water, position himself where the fish were located, and place an attractive offering in front of the scaly critters he was trying to catch. Doug spent all of his time preparing, purchasing, organizing, reading, and talking about the activity, but he never spent any meaningful time actually doing it. No one ever caught as much as a minnow by reading about it, talking about it, or watching others do it on TV. *You can't catch fish without going fishing.*

Stacy's official title was Business Development Manager. Unfortunately, the only thing that she managed to do was stay busy. Either she ignored it or nobody explained to her that her title was just a fancy way of saying she was ultimately responsible for selling software programs.

If Stacy wanted to increase her sales numbers, then she needed to go sell something!

She needed to get away from her desk and take a break away from the charts, e-mails, graphs, and conference calls. To realize an increase in the dollars she produced and the resulting larger deposits in her bank account, Stacy's top priority should be placing herself in front of a living and breathing human being with decision-making authority, explain how she can help that person or organization, and ask for their business.

Don't be a poser.
Don't just prepare for it and talk about it.
Actually do it!

CHAPTER 9
THE BIG CATCH

Taylor accumulated a boatload of knowledge at the workshops and presentations she attended over the last two days at this luxurious resort. She especially enjoyed spending time and getting to know her new colleagues. Everyone was so nice and welcoming to the new kid in the company. People offered her advice, encouragement, and open invitations to call their personal cell numbers if she ever needed any help.

The final event for the sales team was held on Thursday evening so that the attendees could fly or drive home the following morning. Taylor was nervous as she entered the ballroom where the awards banquet was being held. She wasn't experiencing an extreme case of anxiety like she endured prior to the first day working her new territory. This feeling was more anticipatory—like wanting to see who or what was waiting for her around the corner. Everything was new to her. After all, this was Taylor's first time attending a national sales meeting.

The awards ceremony began as people finished their final bites of broiled chicken, mashed potatoes, and asparagus and started to dig into their chocolate mousse dessert. Applause cascaded through the room when Jim, the Vice President of National Sales, presented individuals with awards and recognition for their work performed during the previous calendar year.

It was obvious that Jim enjoyed his role as master of ceremony. He hugged, shook hands, cheesed for photos, and showered praise on all who earned recognition at this glitzy event. One by one, the top performers were called to join him on the stage to receive their awards in front of their peers. The banquet room was filled with an air of dignity, glamour, and celebratory buzz.

"The last person I'd like to invite to the stage is actually receiving two awards—the Rookie of the Year award and the Lead Dog award," Jim proudly announced to the packed room. "The Rookie of the Year award is given to the person who produced the highest increase in market share and overall sales revenue in their first year with the company. The Lead Dog award is presented to the individual who exemplifies professionalism, tenacity, and a willingness to lead others by their positive example and ability to produce extraordinary results," he explained. "As most of you know, it's named the Lead Dog award in reference to the first-in-line alpha dog of a winter dogsled team. The lead dog races to take the team to new destinations, pulls the hardest, and is always looking forward—never behind."

"Taylor, would you please make your way to the stage?" Jim asked after a dramatic pause. The room erupted. The attendees smiled and roared approvingly as she sheepishly made her way through the ballroom and into the spotlight to join her VP. She knew that she performed reasonably well in her first year but had no idea that her efforts produced *these* results.

The tall, young woman flashed a blinding smile and beamed with pride as Jim presented her with the two accolades. The Rookie of the Year award was a beautiful plaque bearing Taylor's full name, and the Lead Dog award was a silver-plated, anatomically correct replica of the south end of a northbound dog with the inscription: "The View Is Always Better From The Front." The awards were big and shiny, and they would look great in her apartment office.

"Taylor, I want to ask you something before you make your way back to your table," Jim stated into the microphone. "A first-year employee has never won the Rookie of the Year and the Lead Dog award. It usually takes a person a few years to produce the results and gain enough confidence and respect to win the Lead Dog award. How'd you do it?"

Taylor thought for a second, smiled, and humbly explained, *"I just tried to keep things simple and concentrate on the process. I knew deep down that if I fully prepared myself to succeed, made a plan, and did my best to execute the plan, the results would follow. It's kind of like going fishing with my dad."*

CHAPTER 10
A FINAL CAST FROM THE AUTHOR

Two years after graduating from the Henry W. Grady College of Journalism & Mass Communication at the University of Georgia, I entered the world of professional selling. That was over twenty-five years ago. During the early years of my career, I was extremely fortunate to be exposed to some of the highest quality and thorough training programs available. During that time, I also had the opportunity to work with and "sponge" the valuable wisdom of a few veteran sales trainers and managers who are some of the finest individuals I've ever met. I realize I am fortunate to have my professional foundation influenced by such quality people.

Throughout my working life I have seen, read, and listened to the latest and greatest business gurus and personal improvement experts in an effort to gain an edge so that I can pad my pockets and provide for my family. I enjoy hearing the different theories, methods, and "secrets" to attracting and obtaining a customer agreement. It has helped.

My experiences over the last two and a half decades have taught me that, unfortunately, there are no 100 percent-certified guarantees when offering a solution to a customer or prospect. For those whose income is directly related to the revenue results they produce, the days can be filled with singing-out-loud-in-the-car highs, fist-pounding lows, delays, obstacles, hope, and frustration. A framed sign that hangs in a friend's office sums it up perfectly. It reads: "Sales Ain't For Sissies."

Catching fish and growing your business are simple activities. Find the fish/prospect, put a bait/solution in front of them, and get them to bite. While it's a simple concept, it can be extremely challenging and downright difficult to get fish or people to react positively to your offering.

A FINAL CAST FROM THE AUTHOR

There are many events that happen in business and in life that are out of our control or influence—decision makers and allies change companies, businesses merge or move, your product line becomes outdated due to advancements in technology, your largest customer changes vendors and purchases from a company owned by their owner's son-in-law, etc. Don't waste your energy on trying to "fix" things you cannot fix. Adapt to and overcome the circumstances if possible. If not, then move on to the next opportunity.

It grates me when I hear someone describe another person as a "born salesperson." No way. An outgoing personality doesn't equate into producing positive sales results. Success comes as a result of preparation, hard work, and persistence. Pedigree doesn't matter. Attitude, self-motivation, planning, and hustle do.

Bosses, spouses, mentors, associates, or friends can't *make* you want to improve your standing in your chosen field. They can't *make* you to decide to do the things that will help you achieve more in life. Others can't *make* you possess a positive attitude throughout each day and set high expectations for yourself. Those decisions are made between your ears and imbedded in your heart.

My hope is that the stories, observations, and simple suggestions found in the earlier pages will trigger you to make the initial decision or rededicate yourself to put a laser-like focus on **the success factors that you can control:**

- Your preparation
- Your planning
- Your attitude
- Your willingness to learn
- Your effort
- Your work ethic

You—and only you—control these vital ingredients to success.

If you *consistently take action* to constantly improve and become excellent in these areas, it WILL make you more efficient, effective, and productive on your professional journey. It will even help you catch a fish or two.

Tight lines and good selling!

ABOUT THE AUTHOR

Jon Wright is an award-winning salesman with over twenty-five years of experience of providing B2B customer solutions in the health care, marketing, and communications industries. He has trained, managed, and developed both newly hired and veteran sales teams and has helped people achieve their personal and professional goals throughout his career.

He also loves to fish.

Proverbs 16:3

For more information, please visit Jon's website: www.tightlinesngoodselling.com.